My Song of Praise

PALMETTO
P U B L I S H I N G
Charleston, SC
www.PalmettoPublishing.com

Copyright © 2024 by Mary Rosenbaum

Cover design by Eric Stone

All rights reserved

No portion of this book may be reproduced, stored in a retrieval system, or transmitted in any form by any means–electronic, mechanical, photocopy, recording, or other–except for brief quotations in printed reviews, without prior permission of the author.

Paperback ISBN: 979-8-8229-3931-8

My Song of Praise

Mary Rosenbaum

Table of Contents

From My Heart to Yours, Lord:	1
A Song of Treasures	2
A Word of Praise	3
The Great I Am	4
A Song of Thanksgiving	5
Dancing Through the Night	7
Life	9
Grace Made a Way	10
I Am Yours	11
Awake	13
From My Heart	14
Much More	15
Amazing Jesus	17
Grace, Love, and Peace	18
Our Song	19
A Prayer of Praise	21
Love Undeserved	22
My Heart Is Yours	23
It Is Enough	24
A Song of Praise	25
Forever More	28
We Are Yours	29
With You	30

Your Voice I Hear	31
Here in Your Presence	33
One by One	34
Rumpled Feathers	35
Open Praise	36
Your Amazing Grace	37
Even When	38
He	39
I Fall On My Knees	40
God, I Need You	41
As I Live	42
I Will Praise You	43
Touch of Grace	44
Fill Me	45
Time Cannot Hush	46
One Praise	47
Sweet Surrender	48
One Drop	49

From My Heart to Yours, Lord:

These last few months have been amazing
You have been closer than a whisper away
Deep within I feel Your presence
Somewhere inside I hear You say,
"I love you"
I know Your hand is guiding me
Holding me
Carrying me as we walk along
The stars of the night
Shine so bright in the dark sky
Yet Your light is brighter still
It lights the next step
Each step of the way
Others in my path have seen me
Have talked to You about me
Have given of themselves
Have reached out
Have helped make the path easier
Bless them, Lord, for sharing their love
I believe Your promises
In Your power I stand
Your strength is my fortress
Your mercy finds me on my knees
In worship of You and Your amazing grace

P.S. I love You

A Song of Treasures

Sing the song of my heart
That everyone else may hear
All the treasures I have buried
Year after year
The notes come swiftly and softly
As I think upon Your grace
Sweet and tender
Laced with care
You open and expose
All that was waiting there
I recognize the power and joy
That float on every string
I see the years of unsung stories
Meant to worship my King
The Eternal One
That reaches down
The Magnificent
Every chord
A resounding sound
Of Your great love
Without a doubt
No hesitation
The God of creation
My strong and mighty King
Can always
Set me free

A Word of Praise

A word of praise today
A word of praise to You
My Holy Father
Magnificent and complete
My heart cries in worship
"I do."
I will not wait
Till You call me home
I say, "I do" today.
I want to praise You all day
Seek Your face
Feel Your grace
As the rain
Drips from the green leaves
Like twinkling stars in the sky
A reminder
Of Your refreshing presence
After the storm.

The Great I Am

You are the lifter of my head
My almighty King
You are my tower of strength
My present help in trouble
You are my ever ready light
In the darkness
My blind eyes no longer see

You are the place where I lay my head
What a sweet, sweet bed!
Your loving arms enfold me
Bring me sleep
I awake with the freshness
Of a new morning
Painted by Your hand

I walk among the lilies
Yours is the Kingdom
The Power
The Glory
The Kingdom
In which I walk
In which I live
You are the Great I AM.

A Song of Thanksgiving

My mind wanders
To so many places and times
As I meditate
On Your amazing love
It was always more
Than I requested
More than I imagined
Overflowing
Touching areas of my life
That were comfortable and content
Not ready for change
Yet You knew it was time
You reached down
Holding my hand
As life jostled me around
Feeding a desire
To awake within
To Your every loving touch
The building of my faith
The abundance of Your provision
The shelter of Your wings
Your strength within
Your joy unspeakable
Your peace unexplainable
Your Holy Spirit
Teaching me
Guiding me

Comforting me
As I walked
Day by day
Thinking of You
Loving You more
Grateful
That what You
Began in me
Will continue
Until I am blessed
With Your embrace
Face to face

Dancing Through the Night

Sadness
A feeling
A direction
I could cry
Or
Maybe not
It kind of sneaks up on me
Sometimes
Like a wave
Always
Takes me lower
Never higher
Whether from things in the past
or
Things that can no longer be
I can let it dwell
Search through all the files
Follow the path it takes
Wandering here and there
Aimlessly
Only to steal
What has been gained
Through His Holy Name
It is my choice
I will look to God
Who will chart my course

The One
Whose steps I must follow
The One
Who turns my mourning
Into dancing
The One
Whose light I see
On my knees
Praising Him
With all of me
Love and joy
Break through
Each step stronger
Each step brighter
As I let Him
Lead me
Dancing through the night.

LIFE

How I long to see Your face
To worship in that heavenly place
A place beyond what I can see
Come, let us worship the King!

I call upon Your grace
It is amazing
It reaches me right where I am
Right when I need it.

I fall on my knees
I fall on my face
Worthy are You, Lord
Oh, most mighty, the Lord of Lords!
Oh, most loving, my precious Shepherd!

Your care
Your faithfulness
It cannot be compared
To anything I experience in this earthly realm

You saw me.
You cared.
You gave.
Life.

Grace Made a Way

I know I am not worthy
To receive this gift of grace
No goodness that I have
Can deserve such great love

It amazes me
It breaks me
I feel Your touch
Reaching through the darkness
Of my sin

The strength of Your touch
Your hand upon mine
Bring tears of joy
As I see Your grace
Make a way for me
Unhindered by my sin
Washed by Your healing blood

I Am Yours

Blow Your wind
Upon my face
Help me sense
A taste of grace
I long to feel
Your firm embrace

I am Yours

You are here for me today
To show Your love
Come what may
Your work in me
Will never end
Only stay

I am Yours

May You lift
The veil for me
Just a glimpse
Is all I need
To see Your hand
Guiding me

I am Yours
From here to You
Is not so far
As raindrops fall
Upon my heart
The light shines through
 I see You

I am Yours

Awake

I awake to Your creation.
I breathe the spirit of Your presence.
As the white clouds hang in the blue sky,
As I walk amidst the tall trees,
I sense the greatness of Your power.
It causes me to fall to my knees.
As I touch the dirt,
As I feel the pebbles on my fingertips,
I am humbled.
Oh, the majesty of Your love!
Oh, the wonder of Your grace!
The song of my heart
Has found a resting place.

From My Heart

I just want to write
Something simple,
Something from my heart.
I just want to write
Of Jesus
And His hold upon my life.

As I think of Him, I feel warm inside.
His presence is real. His love is true.
He's always there when I look for Him.
When I don't, He still is there.

Jesus is a friend and an anchor.
He's all I need, He's everything.
He holds me up when I'm falling down.
He puts my feet on solid ground.

Teach me Thy will, and I'll try to go
Wherever You lead, whenever You do.
Teach me Thy will, not mine own, O Lord
Speak to my heart, "I'm listening now."

Help me to write this upon the lives
Of those who need, of those who know
How Jesus Christ is the only life.
He offers His life for you and me.

MUCH MORE

I had my plans
You had Yours
How we got here
I am not sure
One note at a time
I tried to play the melody
The notes did not harmonize
As I tried to take the lead
Each verse of this song of life
Has found me on my knees

It's Your rhythm
It's Your time
You alone
Know how to sing this song
You have so much planned
Much more than I can imagine
Much more than I need
Almighty King
You have given me everything

There's a melody of completeness
A melody of sweetness
With every chord You touch my heart
Your fingers play
The notes of love and grace
As the angels sing alleluia

Let me rest and be still until Your love
Reaches a crescendo
Through my veins
Until I see You
Face to face

Amazing Jesus

How amazing is Jesus! I love reading about Him and seeing how He changed so many lives. He is my Alpha and Omega, my beginning and my end. I don't know when that end will be on this earth, but I have a heavenly home where I will live forever with Him.

There have been some rocky times in this life – times when I did not know how to keep going, times when I was just hurting, and times when I was afraid because I could not see tomorrow.

One thing I declare right now is Jesus was there each time. He took my hand, lifted me up, and set my feet on a solid plain path. How I praise Him! My heavenly Father washes me with His love and gives me a fresh anointing every morning. I feel His Holy Spirit. His presence is real.

May I follow Your way, Lord, and not my own. May my walk be what You had on Your heart and mind. May Your joy and strength in me encourage others now and later. May my life be a witness of who You are and want to be in a simple life surrendered to You. Keep me close, I pray.

Grace, Love, and Peace

In this place
There is grace
I look upon an image of Your face
I wonder, "How can this be?"
Only by Your amazing
Grace

One moment without You I cannot face
It would be more than I can take
Oh, Your love
How can it be?
You think of me
Reach for me
Pull me close
Hold me
Love

It sets me free
You in me
Walking
Talking
In the stillness of the night
In the torment of clashing waves
I am reminded of Your presence
Deep within
Peace

Our Song

If my words could be music
I wonder what You would hear
I would want it to be
The sweetest love song
So You would know I am near
One language made only for You
A whisper, a fragrance laid at Your feet
A gift to You of all the melodies
Stored up in me

As I stand on the top of this mountain
On this cliff with all to see
The air is crisp and cool
The land is vast and wide
With flowers blooming on every side
One horizon reaches for the other
Clouds hang in the blue sky
As far as the eye can see
The sun is bright with strength
Only softened by the trees beneath

There is no way to describe
What is at my feet
I am startled by the soaring eagle
Who glides on and on in peace
It takes my breath away
The mountains climbing
The winding streams
The boulders huge and strong

I realize that I belong
In all You share
Because You care
Your song of creation
Plays on the strings of my heart
Without a word
You draw me in
Our song

A Prayer of Praise

I come for refuge
Under Your wings I find shelter
I find favor in Your sight
How glorious is that!
You comfort me
You show kindness
In every place
Where I am

I lift my hands to You
In worship of who You are
I sing a song of praise as I remember
All of Your goodness to me
I feel Your love strong in my heart
I desire to know You more
To be as one
In my actions
Words
Thoughts

May I walk with You
Step by step
Moment by moment
As long as this life goes on
Until You call me home

Love Undeserved

I want to love You
In ways I've never done before
My heart is crying
Please, open the door
You have given so much
Yet You want to give me more

May Your voice within me
Unlock the fullness of Your love
As I treasure every promise
Given from above

Make me ready, Lord
Strip away what does not belong
Your sacrifice for me
Is hard to understand
My life becomes an altar
For Your nail scarred hands

The power of Your presence
Pulls me softly to my knees
As I wait in expectation
Of Your holy power on me

My Heart Is Yours

You are the One with whom I want to share my love and my life. I want to draw hearts of love for You and let my life beat for You forever.

From the very beginning You have loved me. You placed me in a home where love was never scarce, a home where Mom and Dad valued Your teachings. They knew the importance of being thankful, of kindness, and a good day's work.

Along the way You blessed me with brothers, sisters, sons, daughters, grandkids, and others who have helped me rejoice and draw closer to You.

Your words brought smiles to my face, made light shine in the darkness, and brought peace to my soul.

Your love changed my life long ago. I am Yours. You are mine. We belong together - Your heart in me, mine in Yours.

As Your love songs flow through me, I will remember Your loving kindness. I will lift my hands. I will bend my knees. I will place my heart at Your feet.

It Is Enough

I am here, Lord
Waiting
Hurting
Wanting to know You more
What is the next step
What do You want to tell me
What do I need to see
I am seeking and listening
For Your still small voice
Is it just around the corner?
Is it right here as I speak?
I'm on my knees, I'm on the floor
I need You more and more and more
Come today and every day
Take my hand, lead the way
You alone will understand
I cannot climb without Your strength
The path ahead is very steep

Let me sing, sing, sing Your praise
Your presence here, Your saving grace
It is Enough
Step by step, I'll make the climb
Filled with Your love
The victory is mine

A Song of Praise

I want to praise You
With all that I am
With all that I can
Melodies of long ago
Of yesterday
Of today
Play upon my mind
As I think of Your almighty plan
To embrace this world of man

Time and again
The songs play on
To give peace
To give joy
To guide
Through everyday life
That I might know
The depth and breadth
Of Your love

I want to walk with You
Walk in Your Spirit
Walk in heavenly places
My Master, my Guide

I want to stand on Your promises
Trust in You
Wait for You
Knowing that what You say
You will do
You are able
My Sustainer, my King

I want to just sit awhile
Soak in Your Word
My meditation is sweet
My Strength, my Redeemer

I want to talk with You
Knowing that You have called me
To be Your friend
Knowing that You Understand

You came
You died
In my place
On a tree
That did not sparkle
Glitter or
Shine

It was a lonely tree
Of darkness and scorn
It was finished
It was done
Through the darkness
Came the light
The Giver of life
From the agony of that day
Arose my Lord, my Savior
Today and forever

Forever More

Is this a song of praise to You?
I want it to be
I want You to see my heart
Feel the rhythm of each beat
Dance with me
As You hold me close
Feel my joy in knowing
That I belong to You
That You see me through and through
Yet You love me

You call me to better places
Places I have never known
Where I would never go
Were it not for You
You go before me
You prepare the way
You prepare me
It's what I need
What I want to believe
Your hand in mine
Always near Your side
Let's dance for a while
Upon this floor
Cherish each time
Forever more

We Are Yours

Oh, my Father
You are my King
You are my Lord
You are the love of my heart
You are the One who
Placed that star in the heavens above
So that we might find You
Worship You, and
Forever be changed
May each journey we take
Lead closer to You
May each song we sing
Express the life You give
May what we do
Show the hope You bring
Touch our world
Speak Your truth
We are Yours

With You

With You I can go on.
My steps are strengthened.
My feet are steady.
I look beyond the things of this life,
The things that shield Your face
And pull me slowly, slowly
Until You reach for me in Your mercy.

Your love dispels the weight.
Your touch brings something new.
You call me to walk with You,
To be refreshed in Your goodness,
The flowers of the morning,
The sun of midday,
The stillness of night.
With You I have the hope of tomorrow,
Rest from the past, and
Joy for today.

Your Voice I Hear

What confidence
To belong to You
Your voice is near
That I might hear
And walk in Your ways
Obey
Serve
You only
Everywhere

In places where buildings are tall
The cement hard upon my feet
People coming and going
With no time to meet

In places of silence
Lofty mountains
Gently rolling meadows
Winding streams
Trees that touch the sky

Your blessings overtake me
You bring good
To everything that concerns me
My enemies run before me

Your holy promise
Forever mine
Your good treasure
Open before my eyes
Rejoicing
You give
Give
Give
Your Word ever before me
That all may see and receive

Here in Your Presence

The day starts with a song
It goes on and on
As You take me into Your presence
High and lifted up
You pull me close
Hide me with Your love
Up…Up…high above, high above
Beyond all
Beyond all my eyes can see
Beyond all that is beneath
Beyond all that is between me and You
My Savior and my Lord

You once walked here
Where I live
A glimpse of heaven on earth
I see wholeness in the broken
I see strength in the weak
I see healing in the wounded
Peace on every street
Life with kindness, not regret
Serving and giving
With never a loss
Heaven comes down
Fear has no place
Only love and grace

One by One

One by one they came
Admitting their need
Declaring You as Lord and Savior
For the rest of their lives
Some were adults
Some were children
Some of one race
Some of another
All in need of Your amazing grace
As they came out of the water
Hiding their joy was not an option
All could see their faces a glow
Trusting in You
For now and beyond
Joy filled my own heart
As I thought of all these
Children and adults alike
Walking with Jesus
For the rest of their lives.

Rumpled Feathers

My feathers were rumpled
My wings were shattered
You took me in and
Smoothed my feathers
You balanced my wings
You gave me strength in my legs so I
Would not sink knee deep.
You put a song in my heart
With dreams from afar.
I am awakened with love
And a fresh new start.

Open Praise

I thank You for the trees so tall
    Makes my cares seem so, so small
I thank You for the blue, blue sky
    The clouds that float right on by
I thank You for the birds that sing
    Their song such a wondrous thing

You meet my every single need
    You are the One who fills my dreams
Now I sing You open praise
    For all the world to see Your grace
It's found within the deepest place
    Your amazing grace!
How I long to see Your face
    Offer praise face to face

I thank You for the stars that shine
    Brilliant in the dark, dark night
You are there when all is lost
    To light the way by Your cross
My open praise I offer You
    In everything I say and do

Your Amazing Grace

Your amazing grace is what I need
To feel Your presence in my time of need

I cannot claim to understand it all
I only know that it's by Your grace
I'm here at all

Down deep You reach into my heart
Until Your blood has covered every part
I see You clearly now
It is not a dream
Your grace has made me wholly clean

A new joy has found its place
With grateful heart and songs of praise
Your sacrifice
Your presence
Your forgiveness
Through it all
Will help me run life's race
By the strength of Your amazing grace.

Even When

Hold my heart for a while
Sense the need deep within
I'm Your child
I am Yours
My confusion, my heartaches, my hopelessness
Touches Your very being

The strength of Your embrace holds me steady
As I sit and think, I remember
You have always carried me through, dear Lord
Even when I brought You pain
Even when the road was rough and
You could see a better way
Even when time dragged on as You waited for me
Waited and waited

You never give up
You keep pressing on
You keep shining Your light and
Leading the way
I thank You, Lord
For this life you bring
For every song that my heart sings

He

He will meet you where you are
No matter how deep the hole
He will find you
He will call you
Listen to Him
He will be your light
To guide you through the darkness
He will be your strength in time of need
His hand is steady
You will not fall
He stands tall for you
He will be your all

I Fall On My Knees

Broken pieces are all I have to give to You
I've traveled this road and am weary from it all
I need Your strength to keep walking every mile
There's no way without You at all

I fall on my knees and thank You for the grace falling on me
I fall on my knees and know Your Word is meant to strengthen me
Holy Father, I'm so thankful You are here
I praise Your name and call on You
The power of Your love is in my face
I cannot deny Your saving grace

You are my all in all
My King of Kings,
My Lord of Lords
My Prince of Peace.

God, I Need You

God, I need You
God, I love You
Stay close by me
Ever near me

I will praise You
Holy Father
I adore You
Prince of Peace

As I Live

Lord, I love to call Your name
It brings promise
It gives hope
Jesus
It makes me smile
Knowing that You are there
That You are here within me
Strong, secure, bright
Faithfully healing me
Constantly loving me
Giving me treasures
To hold close to my heart
Guiding me on the path of light
I'm leaning into Your presence
Rejoicing in the shelter of Your wings
I will take flight some day
Let it not be only then, Lord
May I now sail the seas
Walk the promised land
May my spirit soar to realms above
As I live, refreshed in praise to You

I Will Praise You

Jesus, my Lord
Jesus, my Friend
Jesus, my Hope that never ends
I will praise You
I will praise You
I will praise You
For all time
I will praise You
I will praise You
Your Word lives across the ages
And today within my heart
I will praise You
I will praise You
Holy Father, Holy Lord
I will praise.

Touch of Grace

I fall on my face
At the touch of Your grace
It is always near
Never far away
My heart is less heavy
My steps are more steady
I cannot lift You high enough
You dry all my tears
Calm all my fears
There are no words
My heart cries out with praise
At the touch of Your grace

FILL ME

Fill me with Your Spirit
Fill me, Lord, today
Fill me with Your Spirit
Each and every day
You are my Lord and Master
There's no one can compare
My great Redeemer, my Savior
You cover my path of sin and shame
With Your endless love that leads the way
You guide me with Your Spirit
Oh, how I know it's true
When Your strength carries me
With power I never knew.

Time Cannot Hush

You are my strength
When life is heavy
You are my guide
When the road seems unclear
You are my light
In the darkest corner
My eyes of truth
My voice of victory
My ears for cries of help
You are the touch I need
When hope is drifting
The aroma of a fresh new start
You are the song of life within my heart
That no words can tell and
Time cannot hush

ONE PRAISE

Praise is lifted up from the deep places of my heart
A song is born and delivered to You from my lips with joy
I sing and the heavens rejoice at Your praises
The earth knows this sound of love and need
May its people from every land find their hope in You alone
Then all Your creation will sing as one.

Sweet Surrender

Fill me with Your Spirit.
Fill me now, I pray.
Fill me with Your Spirit.
Let nothing block the way.

You are my Lord and my Redeemer.
Nothing can compare.
Hear the voice of all Your children
As we lift our hands in prayer.

You're the Comforter and Healer
All my dreams complete in one.
You're the One with all the answers
To my doubts and questions.

I'll love You, Lord forever.
It's not a question in my heart.
You came to love and live forever
Sweet Surrender is my part.

ONE DROP

Something in the air
Makes my heart sing
One drop
Takes me to the clouds
Softly floating above the horizon
So sweet, Lord
Lift me high
Help me fly
Above the clouds
Beyond the darkness of today

Sing Your song in me
Write it on my heart
Play the chords on land and sea.
One drop
Reflects the song
Deep inside
A smile cannot hide
Your joy in me
It bubbles forth
For all to see
Waiting to burst
In victory

To know You
To love You
People of every land
Please, understand
Searching or not
One drop
Take that step
Believe He's close
He sees you
He knows you
He cares

Across the oceans
Over the mountains
Down in the valley
Next door
One drop of His presence
Can help you see heaven.

Milton Keynes UK
Ingram Content Group UK Ltd.
UKHW051944250624
444714UK00013B/579